Affirming Your Success

53 Ways to Affirm What You Want and Get It

by Gini Graham Scott, Ph.D.

AFFIRMING YOUR SUCCESS

Copyright © 2015 by Gini Graham Scott

All rights reserved. No part of this book may be used or reproduced by any means, graphic, electronic, or mechanical, including photocopying, recording, taping or by any information storage retrieval system without the written permission of the author except in the case of brief quotations embodied in critical articles and reviews.

TABLE OF CONTENTS

INTRODUCTION 5
THINK POSITIVE 7
POSITIVE PEOPLE 17
INTUITION AND CREATIVITY 27
GAINING KNOWLEDGE 37
OPPORTUNITY 45
GOALS AND PRIORITIES 57
OVERCOMING OBSTACLES 71
TURNING THINGS AROUND 87
MONEY 101
VICTORY AND SUCCESS 117
ABOUT THE AUTHOR 133

INTRODUCTION

Affirmations are very powerful. They help to guide you and remind you of what you want to achieve. They give you the confidence to feel you can succeed, so you are more committed to do what you really want to do. They help you stay focused on your goal or goals, which are critical to staying on the path to getting what you want.

Often people say they want or wish for something. But just hoping that something will happen is not enough. You also have to reaffirm to yourself that truly want that to happen and you will act to make that occur.

Affirmations contribute to your belief in yourself and in your determination to attain what you are affirming. You state them in the present as if something has already happened or as a commitment to do something in the future, although you express your commitment in the here and now.

You can create your own affirmations, and you are encouraged to do so. Any affirmations you create and affirm can supplement any affirmations in this book.

The purpose of these affirmations is to provide you with a series of 53 affirmations, just like in a card deck with a joker, based on taking one affirmation a day, focusing on it, and repeating it to yourself several times a day – in the morning, at lunch and dinner, while commuting or traveling somewhere, and at night before you go to bed.

When you say an affirmation, state it aloud or to yourself mentally. One way is to do so in a relaxed or meditative state, so this helps to solder the affirmation into your unconsciousness. Another way is to say it with firm commitment; perhaps even look in a mirror as you do so, and affirm that this is what you want and that you will make it happen.

Affirmations are also closely related to the idea of manifesting, such as manifesting money, because whether you are monetizing your book or other product or service, you are affirming that you want to make more money for whatever you are doing. Moreover, there are a number of classes on manifesting what you want in life, from manifesting your money to manifesting a great relationship.

Likewise, affirming can help you in manifesting and monetizing whatever you want. Your affirmation expresses your determination and commits you to making whatever you want to manifest or monetize happen.

Feel free to supplement the affirmations in this book with affirmations of your own. They are organized by topic, but you can rearrange them however you want, such as if a particular affirmation is especially appropriate for what you are experiencing now. Just be sure to do one a day, and feel free to repeat any affirmations that you find especially powerful or that have a special resonance for you.

There's also a picture for each affirmation. You can use that picture to help you focus on that affirmation. Or find other images in your home or environment that you feel expresses that affirmation. Then, as you say the affirmation to yourself, look at the image. It will help to make the affirmation even more vivid for you, and each time you see that image, you will think of that affirmation.

So now begin. Affirm what you want and expect to achieve for your success for the next 53 days, and let these affirmations help you obtain whatever you want.

THINK POSITIVE

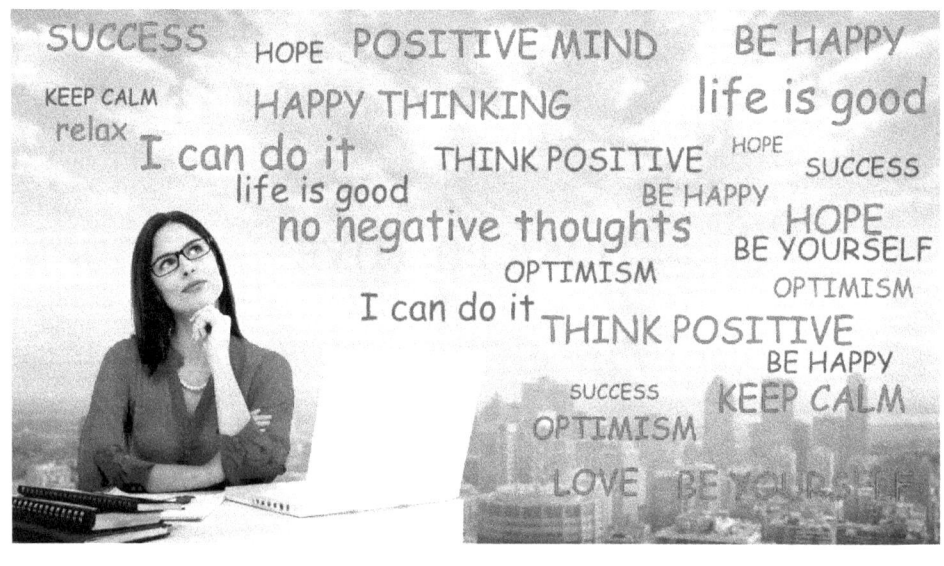

How can I be positive? Let me count the ways.

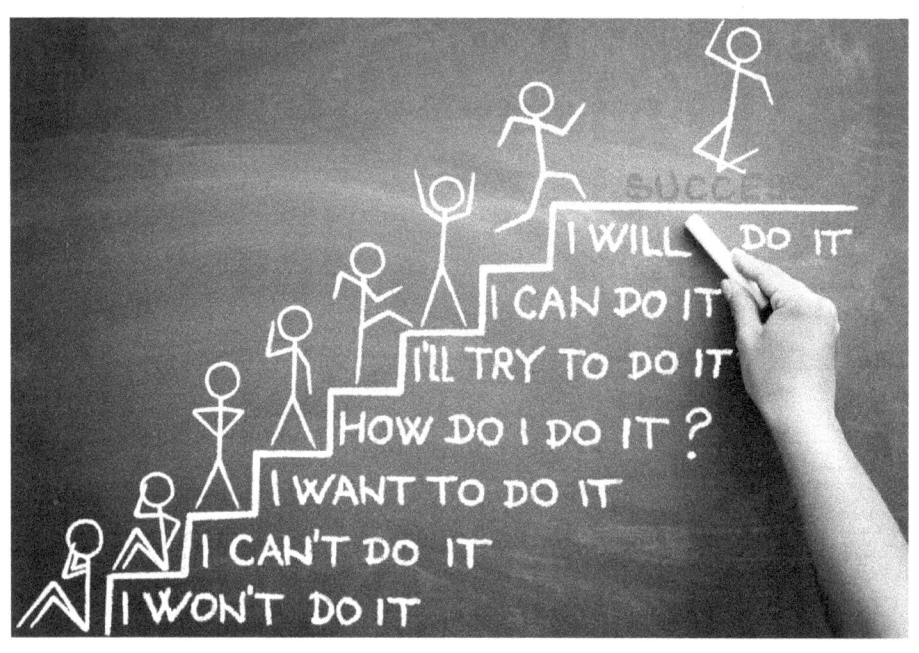

I'm getting rid of the "I won'ts" and "I can'ts," and am thinking "I will" to get to the top.

I have the faith I can do what I want to do. I know I just have to believe, and I can and I will.

I will think positively and remind myself that everything will work out for the best.

POSITIVE PEOPLE

I always seek to stay positive, no matter what happens, because I know positive things happen to positive people.

I surround myself with positive people and put negative people out of my life.

Being with happy, positive people brings joy into my life.

When I help others succeed, we all can succeed, because our success is tied to each other.

INTUITION AND CREATIVITY

I listen to my intuition and let it guide me wherever I should go.

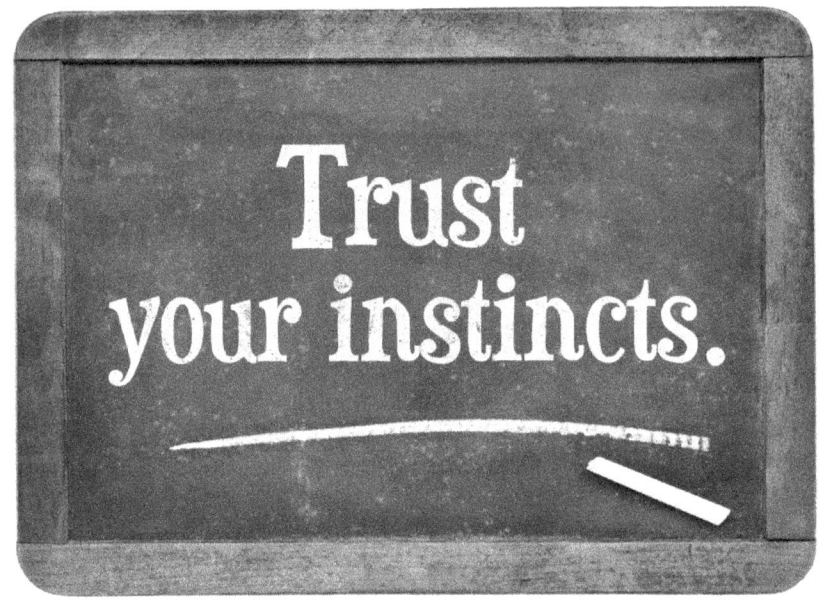

I trust my gut or instincts to tell me when something is a good opportunity or when it is not.

I have great ideas; I just have to turn what I imagine into a reality.

I will keep a journal of my insights and ideas for being successful and making more money.

GAINING KNOWLEDGE

I am learning what I need to learn to become successful in my chosen field.

I have the key to knowledge to achieve success; it will unlock any puzzle of what to do.

I'm eager to learn whatever I need to know.

OPPORTUNITY

I look for opportunities everywhere…and I find them.

When opportunity calls, I listen. And I call up new opportunities whenever I want.

I look for doors I can open to achieve success.

I'm ready to take the leap, and I know I'll make it.

No matter how difficult the road ahead seems to be, I always find opportunities.

GOALS AND PRIORITIES

I have the power to get what I want; with a clear goal, I can get it.

I hold the key within to my own success; I just have to look to find it.

I know my target, have sure and steady aim, and hit the bullseye every time.

I aim for excellence in whatever I do.

I love what I do and do what I love, so the money will follow.

I prioritize what is most important, so I can focus on doing what's most important for success.

OVERCOMING OBSTACLES

When things seem dark and grim, I open a door to let in the light.

Since things are sometimes darkest before the dawn, I always look for a light to shine through.

If I encounter obstacles and challenges on the way to success, I cross that bridge to get to the other side.

It doesn't matter how many turns and detours there are on the road to success; I find the right path to get there.

I clear out whatever holds me back – from possessions to people, so I can move on to achieve success.

If I sense that someone is not to be trusted, I trust that inner warning sign, investigate, and look for the truth.

If I feel doubts, I resolve them quickly and move on.

TURNING THINGS AROUND

If something goes wrong, I think about how to turn this around into a positive opportunity.

If there's a problem, I figure out how to solve it.

I turn the impossible into the possible by thinking of new ways to do something I want to achieve.

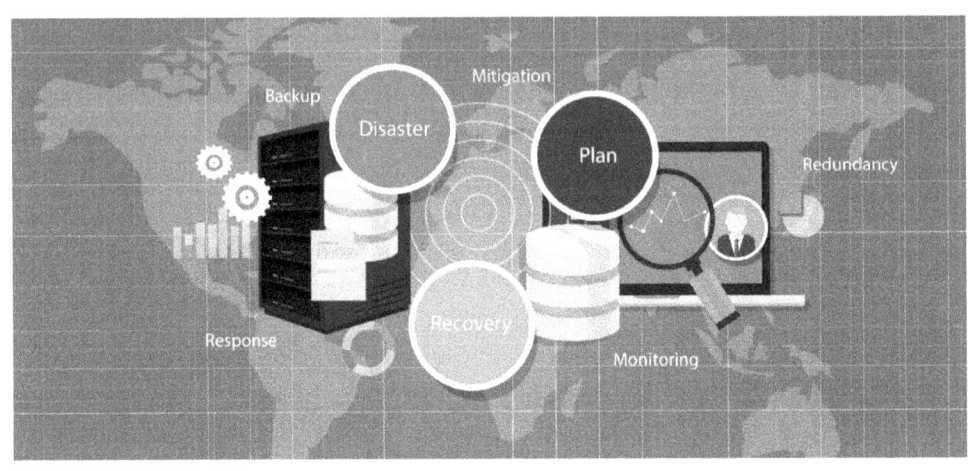

I can recover from anything by thinking of the best way to do so and what to do next.

I don't fear failing, only not trying, since from failure comes ultimate success.

Failure is not an option, because I turn any failure into another stepping stone to success.

MONEY

I am manifesting money, and more and more is coming into my life.

The more I focus on manifesting money, the more it appears in my life.

Whenever I need money, I focus on getting it, and it comes into my life.

I focus on targeting money and success for a few minutes each day to score even more in life.

I am becoming more successful and am gaining more money every day and in every way.

I am becoming financially free; I am on the path to financial freedom.

I look to people who have attained wealth as an example to guide and inspire me.

VICTORY AND SUCCESS

I am on the road to success, and I know I will get there.

I'm on top of the world and know how to climb to get there.

Every day and in every way, I'm getting to the top in whatever I do.

I am a winner! I know I can do it, and I can!

Every day I'm creating my own success story.

I feel great joy, whenever I achieve something on the path to success.

I am victorious in what I want to do, and I'm celebrating my victory now!

ABOUT THE AUTHOR

Gini Graham Scott has published over 50 books with mainstream publishers, focusing on social trends, work and business relationships, and personal and professional development. Some of these books include *Turn Your Dreams into Reality; Want It, See It, Get It!; Mind Power: Picture Your Way to Success;* and *The Empowered Mind: How to Harness the Creative Force Within You.*

She has gained extensive media interest for previous books, including appearances on *Good Morning America, Oprah, Montel Williams, CNN,* and hundreds of radio shows around the world. She is often quoted by the media and her websites include www.changemakerspublishingandwriting.com and www.ginigrahamscott.com. She has about 60,000 listings in Google Search Results.

She has been a regular Huffington Post blogger since December 2012 and has a Facebook page at www.facebook.com/changemakerspublishing.

She has written, produced, and sometimes directed over 60 short videos, featured on Changemakers Productions www.changemakersproductions.com and on YouTube at www.youtube.com/changemakersprod.

Her screenplays, mostly in the drama, crime, legal thriller, and sci-fi genres, include several dealing with changes in science, technology, business, and society, including *The New Child, New Identity,* and *Dead No More.* These are in development with trailers, business plans, and interested directors and talent.

She has a PhD in sociology from U.C. Berkeley and MAs in anthropology, pop culture and lifestyles, recreation and tourism, and organizational/consumer/audience behavior from Cal State, East Bay. She is getting an MA in communications in 2017.

She is also the Creative Director of Publishers, Agents and Films (www.publishersagentsandfilms.com), a service which connects writers and filmmakers to publishers, agents, and the film industry.

Her feature, *Suicide Party #Save Dave*, which she wrote and executive produced, will be released by RSquared Films, in early 2016. Details: www.suicidepartyfilm.com.

CHANGEMAKERS PUBLISHING
3527 Mt. Diablo Blvd., #273
Lafayette, CA 94549
changemakers@pacbell.net . (925) 385-0608
www.changemakerspublishingandwriting.com